In the Library

By

James W. A.

I dedicate this book to my Grandfather, Anthony Mugno.

Even though he isn't in this world to read this, I hope he could be proud of what I've accomplished through living as myself and having no regrets.

Contents

Note on the Second Edition

It's hard to believe it's been almost a decade since my first book, *In the Library*, was released. In that time, I feel like I've grown significantly as both a writer and as a person and I've sometimes thought about releasing a completely revised version of the story written under the experience gained from this growth. This edition, the second edition of *In the Library*, is not that.

Truth be told, I've also often thought about completely burying this first book of mine and pretending like it didn't exist at all. I have Sara Mae to thank for reminding me that this book and its story still have merit after all these years and that it is indeed worth preserving. Thus I am taking the opportunity presented to me by Willheart Publishing and re-releasing it with some slight modifications to bring it into line with the standards of the label.

The vast majority of this text has been unaltered from the first edition to maintain the integrity and tone of the original. To make the book overall more aesthetically pleasing however, the font has been changed, titles have been bolded rather than underlined, and line spacing has been uniformized. Additionally, the key logistical copyright pages and table of contents were absent from the first edition, so they have been added for security and accessibility. The cover and exterior, while bearing the same image and text as the first edition, have also been modernized.

The most notable addition to this edition is the inclusion of the original poem that I wrote as a stand-alone piece that inspired *In the Library*. This poem was released officially on my website as a sort of behind the scenes look at the creation and evolution of the text, and I thought it worth including here too for all to enjoy. I will let that section speak for itself, but this poem, one that bears the same name as the final book, was sort of the origin point, the "concept art" if you will, that eventually evolved into the full book you know today.

In the Library is an important part of my journey as an author and I'm proud to re-publish it now under the label of Willheart Publishing. It is my hope that you enjoy this story as much now as when it was first released and, if this is your first time reading it, embrace it as a part of my authorial canon. As I've signed numerous times and echo again... enjoy the madness!

Introduction

When I was twelve years old, I grabbed a beginner's book of poetry off of a forgotten library shelf and took it home to read and experiment with my new fascination. As the years went by and that book returned to its shelf, I began to read other books and works and explore the miraculous world of poetry proper. I was inspired in deep places by such poems as "The Highwayman" by Alfred Noyes and works of Lord Alfred Tennyson. I grew to love the free-flowing style of John Milton's blank verse and William Wordsworth's appeal to the language of the common man. As I read, I also wrote, expressing my sometimes intense feelings in poetic form, writing almost every day on a variety of subjects. When I had read about the post-modern movement and its manipulative use of language, I knew I had found a literary haven.

Now, a young adult, I have embraced free verse as not only my personal favorite modality of the literary wonder we call poetry, but as one of the most effective means of conveying the message of poetry. Free verse gives the writer the ability to present his or her emotions, ideals, or ideas in such a way that is not constricted by the predetermined constructs of other poetic forms (Gwynn 33). As its name implies, it gives freedom for the writer's creative expression. Moreover, free verse also opens the door for any reader to be able to understand a poem and glean some kind of meaning from it. These meanings can be incredibly diverse because, as some literary camps believe, it is up to the reader to discern the meaning of a poem for themselves (Siegel 10). However, this is also not to say that free verse brings chaos; on the contrary, there is an illusion of order within every line in a free verse poem that is simply unpredictable by the reader, but not without meaning or structure (Kirby 196).

To provide an analogy, free verse in poetry is like light shining through a prism. Think of the image provided in the album art for classic rock band Pink Floyd's *Dark Side of the Moon*: a rainbow prism with light shining through it. The poet creates a work, and by doing so, expels metaphorical light. The prism is the poem itself and the act of the light hitting the prism is the reader's internal analysis. When the light comes out of the other side, however, its expression is that of a rainbow. In the analogy, a reader can intently read a poem and gain numerous different meanings from the one piece, different perhaps than the poet's (the light) and different from others. Because of this notion and the power granted to readers through the idea of a reader-response theory, any person can pick up, read, and enjoy poetry (Siegel 10). In fact, I believe that all people should read and divulge meaning from poetry, and it is a form of art in and of itself (Holcombe 1).

Numerous contemporary poets, including two of my favorites, E.E. Cummings and bpNichol, have written in this free verse style and embraced the freedom of expression it brings. These and other poets like them, who have written within the last few decades, exemplify the same kind of free verse style that I wish to emulate. For example, E.E. Cummings wrote a poem called "I Will Wade Out," that is expressed as follows:

i will wade out
         till my thighs are steeped in burning flowers
I will take the sun in my mouth
and leap into the ripe air
        Alive
          with closed eyes
to dash against darkness
        in the sleeping curves of my body
Shall enter fingers of smooth mastery
with chasteness of sea-girls
         Will i complete the mystery
         of my flesh
I will rise
    After a thousand years
lipping
flowers
    And set my teeth in the silver of the moon

Traditional poetry often follows a set format, but this one is much different (Johnson 4). The lines are not necessarily straight through, but seem to be "split". Also the lines themselves do not necessarily start on the left indent as one might expect; they are staggered out. This is an excellent example of manipulation of form which free verse grants the poet (Gwynn 3).

Another master of the craft, bpNichol also experimented with all kinds of different forms, including some visual renditions. His untitled poem that appeared as the first poem in his book *Art Facts* exemplifies his playful relationship with free verse:

bird and
                breaking the clear calm
beaver's head
                    over the water
i'm glad to see you
                      walking this
held out his hand
                  green & foreign land to be
living in troubled times my mind fills quickly
too much to say
                your brown skin and dark eyes
too many friends being hounded to death by
this sickness

thot we'd raise jerusalem here

ripple this surface with the wind

Since free verse is anything that the author wants it to be, even the rules of grammar aren't necessary. Nichol abandons the rules of capitalization for beginnings of lines and proper nouns, such as Jerusalem, as well as punctuation. Of course, this is completely up to the discretion of the poet and his or her individual style. That is the point of free verse though; it is incredibly flexible in that regard.

It is in this same spirit of unrestrained and innovative poetry that I too leave my mark on the poetry world with my collection of poems in narrative form: *In the Library*. The idea for this project was born one wintry night from what can only be described as a nightmare. A single poem was crafted soon after that night, one that bore the same name as the book does now. Although that original poem remains unpublished for now, from then, many of my negative emotions, and from those I've met, have helped shaped this work and evolve it from a single poem into a complete narrative. When I was given the opportunity to truly hone my craft, what is now this book was forged as my Honors Thesis during the completion of my undergraduate studies at the University of South Florida, St. Petersburg. Now edited and instilled with all that I could temper it with, I now present the completed and fully evolved story that is my first published material. This narrative is meant to be an examination of free verse, adding another facet of its flexible mode in poetry. Its meaning is legion, some of which are discussed in the Analysis section following the main work. Before you begin reading, I would like to extend the warning that some of the material and events depicted in the narrative are somewhat dark and graphic and could be sensitive to certain audiences. I hope you enjoy reading this narrative and gain new insights from its poems, both individually and overall.

In the Library

The narrative begins with the character of Neil, the speaker throughout the story, engaging on a peaceful walk with his soulmate, Wendy. They begin as they had many times over, walking peacefully and joyfully through the streets of a small city, although this time Wendy announces incredible news to her partner: She is going to have his first child. Though they are both overjoyed, their scene would be staunchly interrupted by the intrusion of a gang of Brutes. These Brutes, who care not for love or beauty, inflict incredible pain to Wendy and Neil, simply to sate their own bestial desires, and thus leave them both in a state of chaos and uncertainty.

Trauma

My story begins in a bountiful setting.
The air was warm as falling leaves;
A cooling wind soothed the earth
In this city of ours, a truest home.
Buildings stood strong, monuments to man.
Trees stood beside our evening-lit path
Through a park, a tribute to nature,
As we walked from one through both.

I was not alone that fateful day.
In one hand, only air flowed through;
Yet in the other was truest beauty,
In the form of her, my regal angel.
Hair billowing soft as the breeze,
Eyes and smile shining brilliantly;
She was my eternal Wendy,

And I, her loving Neil.

We'd walked these paths many times
Over the course of many joyous years.
This venture was no different, I thought;
We crossed flora, blooming as our lives.
For though the sun set on this day,
Ours never would, I believed staunchly;
Blessed to walk, hand and arm
Intertwined as dreams and life.

We passed a number of dusty benches.
But at one, she stopped her stroll,
And asked with eyes of deepest pleading
That we might sit together upon it.
I gladly agreed, with arms wrapped on her.
We sat, but her pulse quickened;
I inquired what caused this change,
And she stared at me with eager smile.

A worried look prompted assurance:
All was well, she claimed, if not better.
For the news she bore was grand!
She imparted to me a glorious secret:
It was more than information she bore,
But the form of our first child,
Love growing inside her womb,
Created out of our own.

Elation replaced worry upon my face.
I took her hands into my own

And laughed with the joy of affection.
Tears of bliss welled in both our eyes;
This dream was ours, fulfilled at last:
This family, this world, was ours together.
She laid into my welcoming arms,
And I held her in scared silence.

Indefinite moments passed us
On this beautiful nightly occasion.
The street lamps had freshly lit,
As the pure shades surrounded our park.
We decided to take our leave,
And continue night and life's journey.
I took her hand to aid her up,
And as such, we began our walk anew.

We had ventured not much further,
Smiling with every step taken,
Deeper into this splendid city park,
When a particular chilling wind crossed;
I thought the rustling bushes was this,
Or perhaps the antics of small animals,
But nothing could have prepared me
For the knife then pressed against my throat.

A gruff voice demanded no movement,
But to remain motionless as he was.
As another assailant bid the same,
With a knife at my lover's neck.
It was then that four more Brutes
Emerged from the shadows of the city,

Surrounding us in a circle of sin.
All gazes like hungry hyenas.

Then the Leader of these Brutes
Shown his crooked, vile grin.
I implored for their leaving,
Only to be met with a blow to the face.
My bride screeched, the others laughed.
I asked what they wanted, money or values?
The Leader laughed once again,
They cared not for paper or gold.

More they craved, the Leader cackled.
He stepped forward, not towards me.
With absolute panic, I knew his meaning;
I took my own step in defiance.
Though blades were lowered, it was vain;

Two brutes grabbed ahold to stop me,
And beat me enough to submission.

With look of terror,
                    Wendy screamed,
But not before a brute blocked her mouth.
And the remaining two held her stoic;

The Leader of the brutes took another step
And beat her
                    to the grassy earth,
Expelling her clothes with obscenities,

While spits
                    and
        blows fell down,
Leaving her on the sullen ground.

Then the Brutes,
        each with crudest grin,
Mounted and raped Wendy, my love.

                    Shrieks   cries

                thrusts
    Flashes   terror
                    Anguish   pulsing

Each one exerting ample dominance,
As sobs and tears mixed with blood.
Sometimes pairs performed at a time;

Raging   gagging
                            ripping
            carving,
        pounding
                        The wails,
                                    suffocated
                Dirt and
                            fluids,
    Spewed,   drained,
                    with hellish abandon,

This horrific, most unholy acts,

Until the Leader had the last turn,
Completing with maximum effect.

And when all these Brutes were complete,
The last terror inflicted upon her,
They stood admiring their assault,
These most inhuman of bastards!
And they, with cheers at their dark deed,
Slunk off into the city again,
Leaving her with the totality of agony
And I, the trauma of this sight.

They had made me watch this unfurl,
And I saw more than I could process.
Endless questions filled my mind,
While too many emotions drowned my heart.
Paralysis gripped my wrecked form.
I could not hear a single sound;
No wind across this godless world,
No breath from her broken body.

Was she dead or still alive?
Too far gone or hanging still?
What was to be of our future,
Our child now taken by Hell-side?
My mind was ruptured, eyes bloodied,
Yet one question arose above the others:
How could I process or handle
All the chaos I was now forced to?

After the traumatic events of the assault on Wendy, which Neil was forced to watch and endure, he kneels motionless, trying to process all that has transpired. His mind is swimming with all kinds of thoughts, having shifted from joyous to horrifying in a short amount of time, and he is now left with the darkest of uncertainties as to the status of his future and even if Wendy is alive or not. His most prominent question is this: how to mentally and emotionally deal with the horrors he's seen and how to adequately cope? As he ponders this and an extreme panic attack creeps upon him, a sentient crow appears before him and beckons him towards a place known only as The Library where Neil's pain may be soothed and questions answered. The crow guides him to this building, where Neil begins his journey through the past pains of others, carved into each book inside.

Welcome to the Library

How much time had passed me?

        cold as the earth,
As I lay there,

These grave thoughts filling me,
I felt everything,
        nothing
Within the span of minutes,
           hours,
Or ages,
     it was impossible to discern.

My eyes were gaped,
                    fixed on stars,
As I stared on ravaged knees into oblivion.

Was Wendy, alright,
                    was I?
How could we be,   again,
                    truly,
If there was life in either?
Did it matter?
                    I was too broken,
Hopeless,
            hollow,
                    yet filled deep
With absolute chaos and pain.
I closed my eyes before they burst;
And crumpled to the earth once more.

As mental anguish permeated me,
And panic gripped my ailing body,

I heard a voice call out to me:
Just a soft voice from above,
No angel from a forsaken heaven,
But from a crow,
                    sitting upon a tree branch:
Purest black feathers,
                    with some silver.
I gazed upon it as it spoke to me:

Traveler in life, look up!

I can sense the utter madness,
Infecting you, growing every second;
Born of the joys and horrors
You've witnessed this fateful night:
The ones you did not imagine,
And now are forced to endure,
Although you cannot fathom how.

My name is Gilver, the shadowy guide.
I have seen many ripped apart by pain,
Faced with nightmares they can't describe,
And plagued by the worst of agonies.
I understand all that you feel,
Even if you do or cannot yet.
The uncertainty hurts most, I know:
Now knowing if either can heal or restore.

You are not the first to feel these things,
Even if they seem overwhelming for one.
Countless others have crossed my path;
Upon every dawning new year, more still,
And many more yet before eternity ends.
Each of them I have guided to a place,
A structure where these stories are kept;
The haven of all who know such desolation.

I can guide you there too, Neil.
This aid may heal your afflictions,
Or at least provide you direction.
By learning from those who've suffered before,
You will realize your own destiny;

Cure your madness how you see fit.
So follow my wings as I lead to this site:
Come, Neil, take your place in the Library!

I know not how this crow spoke to me,
Nor could read this despair inside me,

But his words pierced the darkness true;
And if he could guide me to peace;
Then I would gladly follow his form.
Though I knew not this Library,
Or what was contained inside it,
I would soon learn this crow's meaning.

Gilver lifted his wings and took flight;
Flying into the recently-set fog
Appearing through the trees of this park.
I lifted myself up
                    and ran
Onto and through the grass and fog.

He flew swiftly with purpose and cries,
So too I hurried to keep up with him,
As he led me to this unknown site.

We had not traveled long or far,
When the grand building suddenly appeared;
It stood three stories tall, wide as well.
How had I never noticed it before?

I would remember a structure so ominous.

But I didn't care if my answers were here,
Or a weapon to murder the nightmare,
Inside this decrepit abode of knowledge.

Gilver perched on a tree in front,
Just next to the ornate entrance doors.

I strained to focus as he cawed aloud;
The doors swung open, though no wind passed,
And through my pounding head, I knew
That I was compelled to enter inside
And begin my search for answers,
Before the madness overtook me.

We both passed through the portal,
Wood slamming tight behind us.
I glanced 'round the expansive, dim room
That comprised the entire interior:
Countless works filled generous shelves,
On all stairway-connected floors.
The crow perched again on a tall shelf,
And spoke out to me once again:

Welcome, Neil, to the site of Fate:
This gallery of pain, museum of coping.
Please explore the numerous tomes,
As each contains the experiences
Of your compatriots in agony.
Let them speak to you, influence you;
Each will offer the insights you need
To draw you closer to peace or ruin.

Begin wherever you wish, traveler,
And read at the pace you so desire.
Each story will speak to you honestly
And reveal more of human misery.
Stay as long as you require for clarity.
Interact, live, learn, grow through them;
Embrace the panic and obsession,
As you travel, book by book by book.

With a final caw, Gilver departed,
Soaring to the rafters, out of sight,
And I was alone with the undead stories.
I heeded the crow's eerie advice;
With frantic breath and shaking hands,
I scrambled to the nearest shelf.

And with bloodshot eyes, erratic heart,
I reached to open the first of the books.

As Neil opens the first of the Books he finds in the Library, his eyes are flooded with a vision. In it, he sees a man in a blood-stained lab coat over ordinary, damaged clothes, speaking to him against a solidly dark background, with the light showering only on him. After hearing the man's introduction and statements, Neil is prompted by him to read his story that is written within the pages of the book that he opened. So Neil begins by reading the story out loud to himself, mentally processing all that is revealed to him through the lab-coat-clad man. When the story-reading is complete, this man, The Mortician, leaves Neil with a few more remarks in a final vision in which he stands in front of Neil next to the bookshelf, before disappearing, leaving Neil alone with the Books again.

Afterlife

Listen well to us, Neil:
To myself, brothers, and sisters,
Residents of this hallowed hall;
Where if there is any certainty,
It is found in darkest death:
The final form of pain on earth.
Whether you find it yourself or not,
Know it now as I have:

They say tragedy strikes at men
When it is least expected to,
And hurts most in times of order;
So that the darkness breaks that order.

Death has no concern for joy;
Such that when you are driving
Down the highway, literal or otherwise,
And chaos is driving just the same.

One of my hands upon the wheel,
The other interlocked with my wife's:
Such a stereotypical scene of romance,
Yet one without symbolic equal.

Again, Death spurns such symbolism,
And though the workday was long over,

Our ordeal had only begun this night,
When the twin beams drew closer.

The sound of screeching metal,
Was not more terrible than them:
The cries of shock
                    from us both,
Echoing, as our car and future was torn;
Crumpled with dust and pained,
                              flung out.

And through the obvious carnage,
Only two things were evident to me:
I lay alive, the others did not.

The assailant's life had no meaning,
The drowsy worm deserved his demise,

For taking her life,
                    ruining mine.
Yet as I crawled from the wreckage,

                    save salvaging being.
Nothing mattered,

This was a desolate field road,
But her now former place of work
Seemed like a practical destination.

Death is a master with no heart;
Fittingly, it has no beat either.
But it does have a single friend:
It is called grief, a   word.
                    fallen

It is clingy,
           unlike its counterpart;
Enough to fill my mind and heart.

Yet it was kind enough to grant me
The strength to complete my journey.

For grief can be all-consuming,
As it even now threatened my sanity.
Tears formed in desperate eyes
And mixed with blood from scars.
I realized though something about grief,
It can be manipulated, as any principle can be.
The switches snapped in my aching head:

An answer I could face more than this.

I carried her body through field and flora,
As I had held her countless times,
And would again soon towards forever.

As we approached the mortuary doors,
I used her credentials to enter
The empty and eerie building.
This was the first miracle,
                       of course,
But it was not to be the last.

Most people think Death as immortal,
Indestructible and, by men, untouchable.
This isn't the whole truth, however.

A true artist can craft beauty whenever;
And a true doctor can cure any affliction,
With motivation, means, and expertise.

And I could do exactly as I aimed,
To siphon light out of this tragedy.

In this facility, I had a coat and tools.
My process began with needles and scalpels,
Powders and fluids, scattered across the lab.
She had taught me well, a mutual regard.

Only tilted neck and pale complexion
Took away from her bountiful beauty.

And both of these could be remedied.

Soon, my work and mission was complete.
I laughed in joy as she smiled back;
I laughed at Death, its tragedy failed.

Our light, my love, has prevailed!

I carried her home in espousal arms,
And took care of her every day.
We talked and embraced, as lovers should;
No darkness could take that from us.

Though life wasn't exactly the same,
I was overjoyed our story was set.
Sometimes she was silent, as was I;
We could feel our bond especially then,
As all sacred silence inevitably brings.
It was a magical time, as it went on;
My mind strained, but heart was alight.
And Death could not take that from me.

You understand of course, Neil,
We all know loss, even death:
Sometimes literal, sometimes inside.
But you don't have to let it win
If you don't believe in its power.
We can't tell you what reality is;
Because compared to the dreams of insanity,
What significance does life really have?

As Neil closes the first Book he reads, he is astonished and is speechless as to how he should react to what he has seen and read. He knows that its subject was disturbed, but how could he be the judge of that? After all, while his story didn't have a truly happy ending, the man himself was happy, so who was he to question that? While still thinking about what the first specter imparted to him, he almost subconsciously reaches for a second Book, on an adjacent shelf. Still seeking a way to cope with his own pain, he opens this Book and is met with another vision. This one is of a middle-aged man in a brown suit and tilted brown hat, again in the spotlight from above in a dark space. With blood-shot eyes, the man speaks to Neil and, once again, prompts him to read his story aloud. After engaging in minor dialogue, Neil closes the Book.

Obsession

You may think coming here was choice,
But there isn't such a thing, Neil.
Do the hands of a clock choose,
As time moves them onward?
Or do fixated gears grinding
In tandem have such volition?

Either way, Fate moves and reacts
And we simply ride, ride, ride.

The man in the brown suit:
My customers knew me as this,
Their jovial, skilled Clockmaker.

The children loved my whimsical work,
Their parents admired the artistry;
And even in this modern era,
Business was as strong as ever,
As the clocks sold,
        sold,
        sold.

My world was ordered strong.
Each mechanism spinning aright,
Like the machinations I constructed.
Everyone smiled in sequence;
I especially, when these hands
Toiled under creative designing
And expert execution,
As elegant beauty spun,
        spun,
        spun.

But there was another order,
Infecting its way into mine,
Spreading with viral malice.

I began feeling unwell inside,
But this couldn't hinder me
And the order I carefully built.
Nonetheless I sought treatment,
Unaware it had grown,
        grown,
        grown.

Neither dimensions, nor life cared
About the results I received.

Was the doctor lying to me now?
Was this the cruelest divine prank?

The internal contagion was immense
For even the most ordered of bodies;
And Time itself laughed to Hell,
As my own timer ticked,
                    ticked,
                    ticked.

They claimed I had months, maybe less.
But the cancer wasn't most painful:
It was the sting of helplessness

That composed this untimely agony.
Extinction was approaching my shop;
And when it finally came to me,
I knew I wouldn't escape its wrath
When I breathed last,
                    last,
                    last.

I reflected back on what I was;
A whole life of being bullied by Fate.
I couldn't stop my parents' leaving,
I couldn't save any hurting friends,
And I couldn't still my imminent demise.

The shop was damned as I was,
For a life of pathetic weakness:
The horrors that wouldn't stop,
                    stop,
                    stop.

I wouldn't fail ever again.
That image I felt of myself:
A broken man, worthless, dying,
Plagued by what he couldn't fix.
Though my time was fading fast,
I could repair all in my shop.
And craft clocks that would survive
Long after I'm gone,
            gone,
              gone.

I bolted the door, sealed it shut,
None could enter, few to see in,
Save for the children, devoted support;
Forlorn looks peering, sad tapping to help.
I merely closed the curtains fully.

There was no helping, and why anyways?
My hands spun magic the world would soon lose.
And gorgeous pieces were forged,
                    forged,
                    forged.

Forever there was order then!
I built, wound, glued, nailed,

All of my work, a world of gears
Furiously flowing, endless impulsion;
All contact was latched and I didn't mind.
Only my clocks kept me company.
And in a fever of flurrying work,

I could perish happy,
         happy,
         happy.

You, all who read here, can feel it,
The woe of knowing how the clock spins,
Seeing such suffering and of those close by,
And being forced into foreboding silence.

There is no saving ones like myself,
For any of us trapped, Library-bound.

Don't concern yourself with this;
There is art still in Fate, Fate, Fate.

You can judge me, if you wish;
The folly of obsession consuming.
But all the productive labor
Numbed the chaos inside me.

Is that the comforting secret then?
Medicate the pain with escapism?

Some do, of course, all differently;
Continue and learn, learn, learn.

As Neil closes the second Book, he begins to feel for the first time that maybe there is an answer for how he can manage his own pain. The latter spirit related to him a theory of escapism, so perhaps he could consider the same? However, doubts begin to fill his mind again as he feels something inside him draw him towards the Book next to the previous. He grabs ahold of it and opens, unleashing another vision. This specter is another man, who looks far older than he probably is, dressed in clothes that are ragged and torn in multiple places. He is not incredibly dirty or neglected, but an empty bottle swings from his hand, having just touched his bearded face, and a few playing cards fall from under his other sleeve. The man smiles in a sly sort of way and introduces himself to Neil before prompting him to read his tale aloud. As Neil finishes and hears the final remarks of this Degenerate, he feels even worse about his state, seeing the even blissful escape can lead to desolation, and gasping under panic attacks once more, reaches for the next Book on the shelf.

Degenerate

They say I'm unlike the others;
I'll let you judge me, boy.
Where I'm from and whereyouare,
They aren't so different really.
Wee both haunt dim hideaways,
And seeek what we desire most:
An answer to our traumatic problems.
Jest play along and yee might find it.

Do I need a reason for this
Self-destruction, in the best sense?
Bad day, bad month, bad life;
Madnessss drenched in Southern Comfort.

I care about as much asshedoes,
For my state of deterioration.
Every memory burns my skin,
As they fflicker across this hall.

I don't need a home, notthere;
Just these sstools and tables,
And cheap card tricks.
Nothing to find the lady;

For they've lost me completely:
My queen, my knave, my ace.
Sometimes I glance at them,
Given up too, at the bbottom of a bbottle.

Every passerby haunts me.
As they try so aslhave,
Though mine is gone forever,
And our little knave as well,
Bygone to Never-Never Land.
Their dreams cauterized forever
Inmy degenerate mind,

While I waste awway in rejection.

Did theyeverseem to care,

When they walked beyond the door?
Should I even desire hope then,
As I walk into here every day?
I asked the suits, the Rising Sun:
They just wanted to keep playing.
At least vices care ssomewhat for me,

Though invitation is too, a a gamble.

They may yet see meagain,
Though not recognize the face:
The frown of a fallen father,
And a husband, bearded in shame.
My afflictions can't be ondune,
Though time and drink tempt
A chance at redemption.
In myy wildest fantasies,
Thus they'll flash and flash:
A card, a face, a card, his face,
Smiling in lovve and lonnging,
For ones that could never return.

I've abandoned them cold too,
Like sanity's left me allll alone.

Until Death greets me here,
A welcome friend in this bar.
Untilthatday, my boots lie still,
As my body in dirty coat,
As luck and sobriety leave
With fading parts of my soul.

Is there even a reason for thiss
Self-loathing in guise of coping?
Haunted by the past and present,
Of what I've done and failed to do;
Sins and gins and revelries
Are all I canholdonto now.
Good sip, good pick, good life,
Only laughter until demise.

You could say there's no moral,
That I've lost and fallen drunk.
The house and journey have no mercy;
Though the search can be amusing,
But futile, as is desperation.
But keep playing until the acrid end.
You wwant my aaadvice, boy?
There is no justice, no meaning...

Neil is pleasantly surprised as he opens the next Book to find this vision of a Child in a simple pair of pajamas. This feeling of very temporary relief turns into anxiety once again as the Child begins to cry, and Neil realizes that he must have suffered as well. This fills him with more negative emotion as he questions if anyone is safe from pain, even the young? As if sensing his concern, the Child offers no comfort, but speaks to Neil plainly, revealing his story as Neil reads from it. The Child smiles as his story is told aloud and leaves Neil with his words of wisdom, which are ominously beyond what his age would suggest, regarding his experiences and how he dealt with the fear brought on by nightmares by seeking the comfort of another. Neil begins to tear up as well, feeling truly alone and collapses for a moment before continuing his quest for answers and true comfort in the Library.

Inevitable

Hello Mister Neil,
I'm happy you found me.
I see you're not well either.
I'm with you though, Mister.
Let me share my story with you.
One like yours so that you know,
What is found in the shadows,
Even if unwanted, is inevitable.

Mommy, can I come in please?
I can't go back to sleep;
I'm afraid of...

I had a really bad dream.
Can you hold me,
                    Mommy?

It was really scary and so real!

Thank you, I love you too.

I'll tell you about it, if you want.

Ok, I was playing in the snow.
There was so much of it, Mommy!
It was amazing and fun;
The best I've ever felt!
And there was this Lady with me.
She was really pretty, like you!
She smiled and played with me,
And held my hand in the snow.

But then this storm came by;
The snow was blowing everywhere!
And the Lady disappeared.
I felt very lost and sad;
I couldn't see anything, Mommy!
It was all covered in white;
But I heard this noise,
Like the growl from a big monster.

Then I saw its shape:
It had horns, like a lamb,

But made evil sounds,
And it just stared at me.
I walked towards it;

I didn't want to, Mommy!
But I couldn't help it;
I felt trapped and excited!

Then it disappeared too,
And the storm got a little worse.
But then it settled down,
And I was by a mountain.
That's when I saw something.

I don't understand it, Mommy!

There was this wooden thing,
And hanging there, there was…

There were these people,
A rope around each neck.
And they all looked the same;
They looked like, just like me!
But they were grown up,
And each wearing different clothes.

One guy had a uniform on;
He must have been a worker.
One was wearing home clothes;
Maybe he was a good daddy.

Then there was an old man.
He was wrinkly, but smiled a little.
The last was wearing a fancy suit;
He must have had a lot of cool stuff!

But why, Mommy, why?
Why did they look just like me?

Then I saw that beautiful Lady.
She was standing on a ledge,
And crying for these people.

She cried so much!

Then the worst thing happened:
The Lady took out a rope too,
And put it around her own neck.
Then she jumped off the ledge.

She looked like those people;
They were all swaying dead!
And I felt so alone and scared;
I woke up shivering and empty.

Please Mommy, don't let me be!
I don't want to be like those people!
I don't want to die like them!
I want to stay here with you and the Lady!

Please hold me, Mommy;
Keep them away from me.

The monster, those people,
And all their ropes.
I don't want to be afraid,
Of these nightmares;
If they become real,

Please Mommy...

You see now, Mister.
Nightmares aren't just for you,
Mine were real too.
I had my Mommy to comfort me.
What do you have left?
Just remember, Mister.
Even a child's tears,
Can't cleanse a fallen destiny.

Once Neil regains his composure as much as he can in his current state, he pulls himself from the floor and glances around him. This is when he feels compelled from somewhere inside himself to turn around to the next shelf, after having placed the most recently read Book back into its place. He takes a few paces, until he reaches another bookshelf and takes a single tome from it. Again, his mind is flooded with a vision, this one of a gruff-looking Farmer, who scowls slightly at Neil. After his introductions, Neil reads his story plainly, not fully understanding the scope of it. He questions the man, who explains that through his trials, he merely adapted and fought on, regardless of the hurt or circumstance. As the worn man departs and Neil is left alone in the empty Library again, he realizes that he has not the strength to do this and wonders just how much more he can bear to hear and experience.

The Farmer's Destiny

Everyone finds their way here,
Whether they want to or not.
There is no choice in life:
Just joys and nightmares,
Revolving in endless abandon;
But what you do matters most.
Neil, son, you're witnessing now,
Exactly what you need to handle.

I was a farmer, simple as is.
The land was my love, my home.
My plans were set, majestic routine,

There was rule and it was beautiful
As the country I was born of,
The village I had always known,
And the families that supported me.
My existence was happy and set.

But like everything glorious,
It would only survive in this world
As long as Fate would allow.

So with a smile on my weary face,
Sullied with dirt, but no misery,
I ventured towards the village,
From the farm I called my home
With the crops of labor in tow.

My destiny was to be diverted;
That day the clouds approached,
But this was no natural squall.
For as I meandered through the square,
A villainous roar swept the buildings,
And lightning illuminated a stormy sky.
And from the shadowy stratosphere,

A great Fiend descended to our land.

It resembled a leopard, but larger,
With more menacing features:
Red, furred skin and crooked wings,
Claws and spikes protruding;
Malice filled its feline eyes,

Appearing ravenous for destruction.
And it let out a terrible groan:
To shake both earth and souls.

Many of the villagers fled,
To seek shelter in their homes.
Pretending blindness to the monster,
Would prevent their demises.
I was no such fool.
And if I was to die that day,
It would be at the hands of the Fiend,
Not my own cowardice.

It fixated on me, the remaining stander.
This was to be my moment;
I dropped the sack I was holding,
And produced a blade from my cart.
What was once for protection from thieves,
Would now protect my own soul.
As the clash was to begin,
The struggle of man and fiend.

It lunged at me, claws raised.
I tried to dodge, but part of them connected,
Loosing blood to the ground
And pain into my veins.
I slashed at its hide, it growled in kind;
Claw clashed steel with sparks from blows.
There was no clear advantage,
As sweat and blood sated the earth.

Then there was an opening,
The Fiend's arrogance betrayed.
It extended its reach and stumbled;
Thus I parried the way my father taught,
And drove the blade down its neck,
Severing its Hell-born head.
It cried for a final moment,
And the struggle ended in victory.

I panted, grateful for a life preserved.
And the villagers emerged from their homes,
Now that the Fiend was defeated.

They heralded me their hero:
A brave warrior in turbulent times.
They gave me gold, a champion's prize,
And glory, his undying jewel,
Thus the legend had begun.

But I wanted no part of this,
I was a farmer,   not a hero;
My life was set, I was happy there:
Something they couldn't understand.
The story spread of my deeds,
But only of the ones   external,
My joy was never recognized.
My crops never sold,   my story never
told.

There you have it, Neil.
Pain comes in numerous forms:

Sometimes physical monsters,
And those in our minds.
But however they appear,
They won't die on their own.
It is our responsibility as men,
To cast the blades or plows ourselves.

I understand, Farmer, your story.
Though you are far more resilient than I;
But didn't your obscurity hurt as well?

Neil, son, farmer or   hero,
Whatever my legacy was   to be,
It wouldn't change   reality.
So rather than fighting Fate,
I adapted as I always have.

After completing his time with the Farmer, Neil has even more doubts than ever about if he has the strength to continue his perusal of the Library. He knows he must take some kind of action; he's learned that much, but does not know what will be effective. Nonetheless, he finds it within himself to reach for the Book next to the previous one and opens it. This vision is that of a young woman, about the same age as Neil himself, if not a little younger. She is dressed in nice, but informal clothing and has a few tiny, noticeable scratches and bruises on herself. She smiles sadly at Neil as he begins dialogue with her. Finding little in the way of comfort, Neil begins absorbing her story as he had the others. By the end, he is left with even more uncertainty. Wondering if even his choice for coping was truly his to make, he closes the Book and moves on.

A Ransom-less Prison

Are you going to teach me too?
What action I should take now?

Poorest, Neil, I will try.
However, you should know by now,
And if not, then my lesson shall tell,
That actions, like thoughts and feelings,
Are never simply black and white.
True misery thrives in the gray.

There are lovely colors in this world.
In my family, green was prominent.
Bountiful grass, sparkling emeralds,

And of course, that which men desire:
The fullness of riches in paper.

I grew up blessed by it all.
Only the best for daughter dearest;
Happy as wealthy can be.

My days danced like dreams.
All colors shining rainbow.
I had learned all I needed
From the loving family I knew.
Some called me a proverbial angel.
But I was just the best I knew.
Though propriety was learned,
I felt it part of me regardless.

In times of peace, kindness reigns;
A beautiful banner held high.
But all is put into question
When tragedy knocks on the mansion,
Or comes ever near us;
When shadow-filled clouds swarm
Once fertile lawns and windows.

It didn't have to for me.

What began as a simple errand,
An appointment with the family doctor,
Turned from adjusting my glasses,
To seeing the colors of nightmares.
Although I couldn't see their faces

Behind woolen, darkened masks,
Nothing grand was to occur,
As in a moment, I went blind.

I awakened with pounding head,
After indefinite time has passed by.
The room was dark, only light source
                    Filtered in from below the doorway.
                        Was this a grungy, makeshift cell?
                          Was I taken by greedy bandits?
                            I realize this was my fate now:
                          A Captive to unknown assailants.

                          What a desolate descension!
                          The vibrancy of my home base,
                          Now shrouded in the bleakness
                  That accompanies having all left alone,
                      But you, removed from everything.
                        My home, my family, my world,
                            Now lost in the murkiness,
                        The shame of forced abduction.

Though sight was limited in this dungeon,
I could hear voices from not far off.
Some in my head, ringing relentlessly;
Sowing the despair of giving up,
And believing never to be free in life.
But other voices were just beyond
The door of this prison cage:
The gruff voices of my captors.

This kidnapping was for ransom,
These outside voices revealed.
I had thought this the case,
Given my heritage, I was not surprised.
                        Then something else perked by ears:
                            All but one bandit was leaving,
                        Granting my cell minimal protection,
                        With only the scrawniest of the guards.

                            Hope welled up inside again;
                            If I could just make my escape!
                        Dancing eyes glanced at what they could,
                        And noticed a blessing on the ground:
                            Near to me, laid a single pipe.
                            Metal, solid, yet not too heavy,
                        It would make the perfect tool now
                            To rejoin the light of day-shine.

Yet then my parents' words flooded back:
I knew better than this, surely!
My captivity had robbed my humanity.
Momentarily I had forgotten my upbringing.
I could not hurt this unarmed bandit,
For no one deserved the blow of metal;
And I would never hurt another person,
No matter what the circumstances demanded.

                            Would it truly be so wrong though?
                            It's escape for self-defense, isn't it?
I just couldn't harm someone though,
It would just be unfair, immoral;

Even if they did deserve it, in every way.
I wish I was strong enough to help myself.
But haven't I learned as I have been taught?
The way of peace, is all I know to embrace.

Besides, these captors couldn't be all bad;
They had left food and water in my cell.
Surely this nourishment justifies their safety?
I might even owe them for room and board.

Yet for façade, they shouldn't be pardoned.
I'm still bound, no matter my state.
Yet this is my state, content in my standards;
I can't control what I do not choose.

I dropped the pipe from clenched hands.
The light in me was stronger
Than the urge to escape and harm.
Even as the guard looked in to check,
I smiled in a sad, beaten way,
And rejoined the darkness of the room.
The moral plateau was mine now,
Even in these chains of despair.

Interesting then, isn't it?
Even in the coldest of confinements,
The whiteness of ethical passivity
Overcomes the blackness of dubious action;

So that this gridlock in my head,
Of giving up for what I believe in,

And not truly accepting the role I chose,
Is the most haunting prison of all.

You see it now, poorest Neil?
Nothing is free, nothing is chosen,
Not when our minds control destiny.
I truly wish to comfort you,
And I am sorry that I cannot,
But I can't grant you any peace
If it does not exist in yourself,
If indeed such peace exists at all.

Filled with flourishing feelings of uncertainty, though still desiring to witness more the Books have to offer, Neil continues his perusal of the Library. Action, inaction, coping, strength... so many words and ideas fill his racing mind as he stumbles to another shelf. Drawn to a black and gold book, he takes it from its place and opens the tome. Like with the others, Neil is starkly met with a vision of the Book's spirit: An attractive woman, early 30's, wearing a two-piece business suit. She smiles mischievously, as a creature on hunt would before the kill, and extends a hand to shake Neil's. Neil, though on guard, moves to return the gesture, when the woman pulls away and begins speaking to him. Taken aback, Neil then begins reading the story, at the prompt of another waving hand. After he finishes, Neil becomes enraged that one of the sufferers also promotes suffering. He is met with no sympathy, and is instead laughed at again, with the warning that the madness of pain is not only cyclical, it is contagious and relentless. Overwhelmed and wishing this only to be done, he slams the book shut and walks away from its shelf.

Ground Zero

Ha, just look at you, Neil!
Squirming, crawling on these forsaken floors.
Do you want my sympathy?

I have none, pity nor heart.
Do you want to know why?
Everyone, ha, has their own story;
You've figured that out by now,

We've all been shattered just the same.

Fire

Ha

Flood

Quakes

Whirlwind

Many people see it;
Beautifully blazing, consuming,
As it destroys without discrimination.
Simply tearing, ravishingly ravaging.
No heart, no soul, nothing to slow.

I question this ruinous method.
If disaster is truly so unfeeling?
Is it as cold as its blizzards?
Or does something darker dwell within?
I never wanted to learn that secret,
Nor did I expect to understand.

Ha, I cannot lie now though:
Disasters clearly   enjoy desolation.
I didn't believe it either until
It played its sinister game with me.
Another productive day at the office,
While the savage quake rocked my home,
Loosing open flames upon all within;
Eradicating every   thing in eruption.

How inhuman this calamity was!

Cruel
Sadistic
Covert
Thorough
Thieving
Ha

How unnatural disaster can be!

To prey upon one so established,
There was no reason behind brutality.
Nor could I have expected,
The earth to   starkly catalyze
The ruination   of all I had:
Years of work   and prosperity,
Now obliterated and obsolete,
All home possessions now taken.

I could see into this cataclysm.
It didn't just sweep without warning,
This devious disaster enjoyed,   lavished in
Every item and comfort it took,
Secretly laughing as it absorbed them.

This maniacal   misfortune savored
My misery as it compounded,
To petered pride and wounded wallet.

Do you want to know how,
I can accurately personify here?

I am exactly the same way!
An adversity all of my own,
Or at least the herald of one.

For all the worms creeping below,
From my perch high aloft,
This managerial   throne of mine;
Every day they curse my wrath,
As I flood it over these underlings:

Shouting
                Demanding
Bemeaning
                Ha
Chastising
                Dismaying

I write the domain's power,
And they beg not to see it.
But after enough encounters,
Their dignity   is so tattered,
They believe they are as worthless
As I impart to them regularly,
And deserving of every sting
I inflict on their senses.

To bolster my own esteem,
None are spared from   glory's
storm.
My own little boy was caught in the tempest;
I slaved him for company and self,

with words of   choicest callousness,
    Subjecting him to the whims of my appeals.
And, ha, how his   life-mind was wrecked,
        Turmoil I cared nothing for.

What's more,   every joy I take,
    Every peaceful   day undone,
        I grow a little more whole,
        Increase my own happiness and status
        By filling the void and blooming;
        Abundance built on ruinous misery,
        Ha, turning their tears and cries
        Into my own gleeful laughter.

Catastrophes took everything from me;
So I took towards everyone's losses.
Such bliss that comes from breaking

Minds
        Hearts
Spirits
        Lives:

The musings of a Machiavellian Manager.

You cold-blooded monster!
It's because of people like you
This cycle of confusion, relentless violence,
Can flourish and expand!

You're learning, Neil, that's good!

The insane infection is also now
Spreading to and through you yet.
We're all strewn along, ha, like you and like I.

But isn't there a converse, a breakage?
Couldn't peace and good will thrive
And be instilled to others instead?
Can we escape the chaos in light?

Of course, altruism is a solution,
I'd be a fool to deny that.
But don't be one either, Neil;
The future is in flames effusive.

Neil takes a moment to catch his breath, it having been on overdrive from witnessing the various visions he has seen from the Books he's opened. With the essence of doom that he gained from his latest encounter, he finds it difficult to read any more, but somehow finds the strength to scramble over to a shelf nearby, where he notices two very similar books next to each other, one blue and one pink. He grasps and opens the first and is met with a vision of a young man, mid-twenties, dressed in casual, urban clothing standing before him. The young man is startled at first, but then proceeds to impart his lesson to Neil, who listens with a curious heart. Neil proceeds to read the young man's story, which is written in the form of a letter to his Twin sister. Upon reaching what Neil feels to be an unsatisfying conclusion, he asks the young man for clarification. The young man then prompts him to read the next Book on the shelf for the answer to that query.

Infliction (Volume One)

You're not my sister!
She's precious to me, you know;
Maybe that's why we were damned.
It's the trusting connections we forge
That catalyze our greatest joys,
But also our deepest pains.
You're here, so you already know
The torment linked to these bonds.

Dear lovely Twin sister,

I've completed what I sought to do,
For you, for me, and for justice.
My actions today and their results,
Have avenged all that we've endured
And everything we lost to them.
They have been sheared of life;
Left with no way to gain again.

I always told you I'd be strong:
The brother you've always deserved.
And this conspiracy I've now burned
Into our history, our legacies;
They have choked on their fried cakes,
Cut down in drunken stupor, thus
Banishing all injustices inflicted,
And forbidding future betrayals.

I have no need to reiterate,
The wrongs that were inflicted on us
At the hands of that loathed Law Firm;
So-called "higher breed" of liars.
When we were injured and vulnerable,
They offered guidance and fairness;
A chance to replay the moments,
That would allow us a fresh start.

But every word was a lie,
Calculated coldly for the sole purpose
Of tricking us into willingly giving
Everything we saved, to these scoundrels.
And they simply laughed and shrugged,

As they consorted with our enemies.

Robbing of us all the wealth we had,
To fulfill their filthy greed.

Even though we both believed,
Their tact allowed them safe escape.
But you know me and my drive;
They wouldn't evade my justice.
No man, beast, angel, or demon,
Crosses against my sister and me.
They learned this the best way I know,
And repaid karma with fatal interest.

I grasped my favorite tool of Fate:
Such a simple handgun, but effective.
Strategy didn't factor in for me.
What do I still have to lose?

The front office door wide open,
As my grinning face sauntered inside.
I disregarded the secretary,
And burst into their brood's meeting.

There was no need for remarks now.
There was nothing to say to restore
The money and dignity they took those days.
Their looks of surprise and horror,
And momentary spike of fear,
Was enough to make me grin more
And chuckle just to myself,

As a bullet implanted each of them.

One shot into each of the vipers;
It was at least something to fill
Their normally hollow chests.

There was one in particular:
The closest, my filthiest enemy,
Beloved disciple of villainy.

He took a bullet to each kneecap
And, as he pleaded on the floor,
I approached, drove the gun inside,
Enveloping eyeball with the barrel,
And fed his vision with a gory round.

After the last bodies fell down

Spitting,
        croaking,
                to the earth
                        they belong in,

My own heart was at peace;
All agony washed away from me
Through the rivers of blackened blood.

Do not fret for my own safety.
I'll do my time with honor.
It doesn't matter how long anymore,
Because the whole world is aware

Of the price for cheating the commons.
So find peace, knowing you avenged,
And justice shall reign forevermore.

Love, your gallant Twin brother.

Believe what you wish, Neil,
About revenge, action, inaction.
You have that luxury now;
Although I still pity your loved one.

Was your sister okay afterwards?
Can you give me hope for that?

Are any of us, our friends, okay?
Ask her yourself if you can manage...

Neil closes the first Volume of the Twins' Books and proceeds to pick up the second of them, lying right next to the first on the shelf. He hopes to gain the complete scope of the story through the sister's insights. Upon opening the tome, he is greeted by the sad vision of the second Twin, a young woman dressed similarly to her brother, but with a sweater and long pants. She begins her tale by conversing with Neil before encouraging him to learn from her story, with particular regards to the nature of the Library as a place of cryptic and unexpected answers through pain, but insights nonetheless. After Neil finishes reading her story out load, the young woman takes off her sweater, revealing the numerous self-inflicted marks on her arms and rest of her bare body. Neil looks for a moment, horrified by the mutilation she brought to herself, but then promptly closes the Book, ending the vision. He breaks down indefinitely, not wishing to see any more.

Infliction (Volume Two)

You aren't my brother!
Oh, he sent you here though?

Your Twin revealed to me
That you could give more insight,
For hope and meaning in pain.
And if your tragedy turned well?

Although skepticism fills me,
As I venture this forsaken place.

Ah, my misguided brother said that?
He's not wrong, I may help.
There is meaning, curing here,
In this Library you call accursed.

However, it is never what you expect
Or hope for in the light of healing.
But often what soothes the storm inside,
Is to fall deeper into numbing shadows.

Dear hardy Twin brother,

It's over for us now, isn't it?
I thought there may have been
Something to hold, material or not.
But Fate is crueler than we knew,
Like that Law Firm, sociopathic,
Who took all that we had accrued:
Our home, our money, and our future.

You told me, you'd make amends,
To protect, like you always have.
But instead you gave up even more:
Your own freedom in exchange for lives.
There is no justice in such a vengeance,

On either side, the good or the evil.
You received your peace and reward
At a price we all had to pay.
Don't fear for my safety though;
My best friend offered me a home.

A sanctuary when ours has crumbled.

Yet even material comfort here,
Cannot cure the void and misery
That has overcome my inner soul.
The pain of loss of all I knew,
And both our own bleak futures.

While despair down-poured on me,
I too found a source of comfort,
In the unlikeliest of mortal ways.
When in a moment of rage and emotion,
I clamped my teeth tightly on my arm,

Holding,
      clenching,
            without restraint
                  or reason.

Until I would stand no pain or blood more,
And admired the sore marks produced.

The sensation my own lashing produced,
Seemed to still the empty chaos in me;
Yet it burned in its own right.
At first, I didn't want this:
To know the sting of self-affliction,
For I knew it only made life darker.
But after every crunch, every mark made,
The despair was replaced with numbness.

It was in this, that I found my comfort.
Escalation soon accompanied me;
As I switched from biting fiercely
To my new favorite tool of Fate:
A small blade from the kitchen counter,
Now etched into my speckled skin,
Each line drawn, cut slicing into me
Replaced a little piece of my hell.

There is a certain calm numbness
Gleaned from mutilating what ails you most.
But isn't physical affliction,
Better than the chains of depression?
Bleeding apathy than panicked madness?
Now that all the agony is washed away,
Through streams of my own crimson blood.

Love, your sorrowful Twin sister.

Look at me, my arms, my form.
Even in affliction, there can be wellness,
A paradox in pain; physical or not?
The foggy dusk or stinging compulsion?

Dear God, why must it all be so?
If your brother, friend were just supportive...

But they weren't, I didn't want them to be.
Sometimes it has to be this way...

After moments of silence pass, Neil lifts his eyes upward once more to see Gilver, the avian guide who led him into the Library, perched on a shelf a few rows down in the building. The bird lets out a cry and pokes the top of the shelf with his beak, as if beckoning Neil to come to read from one of the books sitting on it. Neil hesitates for a moment, uncertain if he truly wishes to continue reading. He decides that more could be useful to him at best and either way would be interesting to know. He struggles at first, but walks over to where Gilver's shelf lies and a particular book catches his eye, for no real reason other than that he feels drawn to it. He takes and opens it to see another vision of a teenage young man, long hair, loosely dressed, looking as if he had been crying. He makes little in the way of introductions, appearing to stare off into space, but motions to Neil to read nonetheless. He leaves him after his story has been passed on, but not before sparring words with the frustrated Neil, who now teeters on the edge of panic-induced insanity.

Word of Healing

You've seen terrible things,
Or heard them vicariously.

We all have inside here,
This Library of pain;
Our realities fractured and broken,
We're cursed by our worldviews.

Let me tell you this Lover's,

From nearly unknown origins,
A tiny spark ignites within;
And for days my body locked,
Inside the grip of panic:
Heart threatening secession
By beating out of my chest,
Breath is indecisive,
Between rapid and barely existent,

And this pit in my stomach,
Is nearly as void as my soul.
I lay strewn on this bed of mine,
Like a medieval rack of torment.

Though I can barely make it
Topside and through the day,
The world still blankets around me,
Smothering with darkened disregard.

No medicine or food can cure this,
Although each remedy I've tried.

Friends and family are all shadows,
If they even care at all.
With midnight approaching relentlessly,
And hope exiting en masse,
I turn to you, my love,
To receive healing from my angel.

Every hurt I pour towards you,
How I feel so alone, so scared, so cold!

Each word, a fallen poison drop,
Moments seem to go by,
Etching across an infinity.

And then I hear you begin,
The voice to bring me comfort:

"Okay"

Moments more pass me by.
I protest more, to this end:

"Okay."

Thus an angel falls into sleep.
I crawl away, pain resumed:
Bleeding frozen, saline droplets,
Desiring only your embrace,
Left horrified by your indifference.

But your image I still believe in;
I have no choice but to sustain it:
To embrace an angel's arms,
In dreams, if not in reality.
For the sake of my fading sanity,
And preserving bound-kept life,

For it is all that can keep me

From kicking the chair away.

Do you understand it, Neil?
Or least you're beginning to:
Reality is cruelest when nightmares are real.

I held to whatever I needed to
To get through the day, my life.

What you choose to believe in,
Is your choice alone to make,
But choose something worthwhile.

Does it even matter what I choose?
Who is truly there to help me?
Could I walk out of here now,
Knowing at least some sanity exists?

You don't truly see it yet, then:
None exits the Library unscathed.
Comfort is an illusion, Neil;
And healing, what you make of it.

As Neil closes the latest Book with anger and places it back onto its shelf, he looks up again to see Gilver caw at him. Neil stares at the bird sadly, looking for either sympathy and mercy, or answers and hope. Gilver stares down as well, offering none of those, but somehow Neil knows that he must read one final Book to complete the lessons that he has been taught thus far. He reaches to the shelf just above the previous one and takes down an eleventh Book. As he opens it, something positive stirs in him for the briefest of moments as he meets the vision of a young woman, tired and worn. Her expression makes no indication of any emotion, nor does it change as she begins to dialogue with the equally weary Neil. He reads her story soon after. Upon hearing this woman's lesson in purest form, he for the first time realizes the scope of all he has read and breaks away from the shelf after returning the final Book to reflect on his entire experience.

A Final Dream for Treason

Can you afford one last reading?
A final lesson in this temple?

My sanity is nearly broken,
But if one more is required,
I will endure your story now.

Thank you, traveler Neil.
I promise my story bound
Will form your journey's conclusion.

Though your sanity may not survive,
This is the nature of pain.
Some things must live or adapt;
Some must perish for survival.

But when all fades or ignites,
Ever questions remain or are resolved:
Do we deserve the hurt we feel?
Do we sow chaos or fall victim to it?

Some say that a personal utopia,
Is living in love with another:
Hand in hand, souls intertwined,
This was the vision I always dreamed;
And I had claimed it with my lover.

Yet as I pen these words now,
Let this note serve the world
As a testament for treason and guilt.

When our story began, joy blossomed strong.
We built a present, a future,
That was stronger than this world.

We believed this with every heartbeat,
Synchronized as our souls had become.

But Time is soulless, uncaring for love.
As is the cold darkness of sleep,
When its dreams arrive like swarming crows.

They struck with ruthless abandon;
One after another, the dreams recurred.

As my lover and I had drifted...

The face of another haunted me...

These thoughts permeated my life....

With every passing dream,
I couldn't fight this infection inside:
The desire for Forbidden Fruit.

Every flash in my mind,
Left a scar on my heart.

Until it could be ignored no more,
And dreams morphed into action.

Fate thrives itself on madness.

And opportunity shines on malice.
When all was aligned in this reality,
I willfully consummated my crime.

When I awoke from sinful passion,
It was nightmares, not militant dreams,

That had consumed me in this way.

Like a white card stained forever,
The love I had built for naught,
Was now tainted by my selfishness.

I write this so all may know
The truth behind the tragedy.

Know too that it is a terrifying emotion,
The strongest of all guilt's,
That now floods my heart and mind.

I would pay for my betrayal
For my whole life, now abandoned.
So I will not live here any longer.

To be left with the guilt I created,
Is less than the Hell I deserve.

The only white card left now,
Is the one containing my last thoughts,
Splattered with tears and drops of liquor
That I take to prepare stinging descent.

As you read this broken note now,
I will be looking up in misery.

My body filled with yellow jackets,
Initiating a breathless suicide.

One pill for every dream,
A poison to match their own.

Ten...

Fifteen...

More I imagine...

A just end for your fallen angel.

Remember me fondly, I implore,
Not as the Traitor I became.
As slumber is the sorrow of lies,

And forgiveness, an impossible dream.

This is the final lesson of our Books:
That for the hurt, the martyrs, the victims,
As well as the guilty and the broken,
Pain is as universal as humanity.

Everyone suffers in some ways,
It doesn't matter how or why.

But these shadows will haunt all forms,
Until by choice or not, we greet our demise.

Now that Neil has completed readings of eleven of the Library's strongest Books, he is able to take a moment and reflect upon all of the stories he has read and the events that he has vicariously lived through them. One by one, he recalls the various lessons taught to him by each of the eleven Book characters and how they have impacted his life and mental state. When all of his recollections and analyses are complete, Gilver calls down to Neil from his perch and prompts him to glance into one final Book, a white one set on a podium apart from the others. As Gilver flies directly above it, Neil complies and is horrified to find that this Book contains his own story, albeit without an ending. As all of this knowledge and emotions storm in his mind, Neil at last falls to the ground on his back and begins to laugh. This breakdown causes him to laugh exponentially and maniacally as he closes his eyes and all memories fade away. When he opens them again, he is lying in the grass where his story began. As the sun comes up, he continues to chuckle to himself as he stands up, noticing Wendy's body lying nearby, but unable to remember or care, he disregards and continues the walk he began. As the sun rises above the horizon, he begins his life anew, happy and carefree, embracing the bliss of insanity.

Paradise Onward

Eleven Books, each a sacred survey
Of the pains that haunt mankind;

I have vicariously lived them all:

Absorbed all their secrets,
Stitched them into my skin,
Etched them into my brain,
And injected them into my soul.

How my own agony has mixed with them!

From the Mortician, his job that became,
I learned that loss is death.

Sometimes literal, sometimes uncertain,
But that need not be permanent
If you refuse to accept its shroud,

And instead craft a world without Death
With a tricked mind and handy skills.

Life is life, even if it is a lie.

From the Clockmaker, king of his shop,
I learned that sometimes deepest pains
Are sicknesses or stoic circumstances,

That no mortal being can change.
And wherever that knowledge leads us,

Or how it ruptures the world we know,
Escaping into a mountain of work,
Can deflect life's horrifying truths.

From the Degenerate, filthy brokenness,

I have seen the stark desolation
Caused by the rejection of those desired,
And the torments of staggering alone.

Drinking and gambling can soften its blow,

The basest form of escapism,
But this only quickens the descent;

The empty bottle, a symbolic void.

From the Child, crying affliction,
I witnessed the terrors of sleep,
In the darkest of nightmares;
Haunted by these swarming fears,

Shadows of what may come to pass.
Yet such tears can be soothed

In the embracing arms of another,

From those who melt the madness.

From the Farmer, once a hardy hero,
I've seen that it is indeed possible
To combat your distress directly;

To face any fiend, external or otherwise,
If you have the strength to do as such.

Or else see all you know and adore,

Fall into fiery ruins as a result
Of weakness and lack of will.

From the Captive, a taken angel,
I've observed what transpires
In the mind of one who is gray.

For even when bound and bruised,
And harboring every desire to strike,

Still the conditioned response of light,
Prevents any active reactions,

And passive gridlock is produced.

From the Manager, ruthless bane,
I discovered devastation from loss

And the gravity of abrupt disasters.

Her treatment advanced the circuit,

As violence does to itself;
The sufferers maim the suffering,

Sympathy is whittled and lost,
And no converse could quell the storm.

From the Twin♂, a wayward brother,

I was told that relationships
Create the strongest links to anguish.

I knew this to be true, of course;

As my own reaping stung in this way.
But as trespasses are done to our friends,

So too we can reap vengeance.

As if it could bring any peace!

From the Twin♀, a misguided sister,
I gleaned that losses come and go,

Anticipating, compounding dread.
But amidst all the misery formed,

Swirling in a compromised mind,
Physical agony, self-inflicted wounds
Can take away from the inner din.

But no scars will ever bring true peace.

From the Lover,
                    lost in disbelief,

I've learned that when all could be grand,

Even supposed love can produce chaos.
And when the ones who care most don't,

The intensity of panic and neglect
Can only burn if you believe them.
When you cannot accept the cruelest reality,

Choose not to live there: choose denial.

From the Traitor, a fallen queen,

I saw the other side of painful feelings:

That when mind and heart
                              become twisted,
And the greatest treason is wrought,

The agony of the guilty one
Is just as great
                  as the victim;

Thus affirming that with all its forms,
No mortal is truly safe in this world.

Thus I know my journey's ending
Is nearly upon me as I speak.

As these truths
                  and consequences
Offer what I from the start knew:
That there are no answers,
                              no hope,
Only more torment built upon itself.

This is the nature of this Library,
Accursed microcosm it may be.

Neil, I'm glad you know this now;
Though I am truly sorry for this time.
There is one last Book you must see
To fully complete your experience
See now where I hold flight
Above this single white tome,
Separate from your now siblings.
Look upon its freshened pages!

Gilver, I will listen and observe,
As my aching
          spirit and tender brain
Draw me towards this final Book...

This text, this character,
          a broken man,

But his name,
      it is my own!

Am I now to be chronicled too?
Become a gear in this horrid
          machine?

A fixture in this gallery of nightmares?

Yes, Neil your journey is done.

Therefore your tale shall be written
And etched in paper forever;
So that future guests in here,
As we shall be open forevermore,
Will learn from your own insights.
This too is the nature of the Library:
The compounding stories, one by one.

Do not fear this, Neil.
Your time here is completed.
Your mind is free, albeit tattered.
If there were choice, you'd make one,
And react how suits you best.

Knowing the answers that exist,
And the destiny that lies before you.
Go, Neil, fly to wherever you can!

I can choose,
        this Book,
                my own,

No choice,
        ha, only reaction,

But the ending,
        blank and empty,

I don't care,
        not anymore,

The ending,
            it is there, or not,

Ha,
     only laughter
                  consumes me,
Each sound, ha, loosing away,

These memories,   my pain
                this life,

        Ha
                  Ha
          Ha
                      Ha
   Ha
              Ha
                  Ha
      Ha

Everything now is gone.

The pain, the joy, Fate itself.
The laughter has drained it all.
I simply lie here on the grass,
No buildings, no lights, no souls.
Just myself, the wind flowing past.
Ha, I have made my reaction clear;
And embraced the bliss of insanity.

I stood up, as the sun arose,

Creeping upon a new inception.
There's a woman's body, unmoving.
Disregarding, I was on my way.
A few more chuckles escaped me,
But nothing haunted me at all.
If I was distressed, it matters not to me,
As I walk onward to a bright horizon.

The Original Poem

Before it was a full-length book, "In the Library" was the name of a single poem that I wrote in January 2014, a little over a year before the release of the book itself. While I took my time building the narrative pieces that would become the full version, these handful of stanzas were written in one feverish sitting, ironically, though perhaps unsurprisingly, in an actual library.

I would like to share this original poem with you:

I stand here lost in question

Nameless books in labeled halls
Countless line this corrupted building

A cry resounds from somewhere
It must be from one of these tomes
After all, one must have my cure

Frenzied by fear and desire
Compromising mental barriers
Running across these shelves
Before I collapse into madness

It has to be among them
These dusty and pristine rogues
Holding the answer that I seek
A weapon to murder a nightmare
And restore idealistic beauty

Heartbeats sync with furious hands
On spines tapped as I pass
And the laughter of phantasms
Trapped within my mind
Desperate for the peace
That comes with luminous love

I follow the echoes here
A title worn, binding stained
Gaped open to reveal
Most pages have been expelled
So only void ones now remain
I shall take this enigma, embrace it
And we'll write the ending ourselves

I'm sure you can see right away how this piece evolved into the tragic tale of Neil and his journey through the mystical place called the Library. This speaker also seeks an answer to a very troubling, yet unknown question, although arriving at a different ending than their protagonist counterpart. When going from stand-alone poem to full-length book, I thought a more definitive beginning and ending was appropriate for the character of Neil, as opposed to the more abstract concept that was this original poem.

Poems, like people, can evolve from ideas to characters to full stories. I don't know where you find yourself in your life right now, but even if it feels like an "enigma," it is your story to tell. So embrace it and write your ending... wherever it leads you.

Analysis

You have now read, and hopefully enjoyed, the narrative I have presented here in this book. It is my hope that all readers discern some meaning from this piece and, in fact, find their own meaning in the story and its myriad of characters. As noted already, *In the Library* is a presentation of free verse. Therefore, it would not be beyond the realm of possibility for each interpretative community to glean different interpretations from the story (Siegel 10). While I certainly encourage each reader to find something in the narrative that speaks to his or her own life condition and circumstances, I still wish to provide some analysis. This will offer a better understanding of the work from the author's standpoint and what the implied reader should gain from it (Siegel 10).

"I have seen many ripped apart by pain…"

There are a number of major themes present here, and one of the most important is the notion of pain and dealing with pain. It is both unfortunate and undeniable that all human beings suffer and endure evil in this world (Jung 21). Just the same, each of the main characters suffers in some capacity. From the opening poem "Trauma," Neil is dealt a heavy blow by having to watch his lover Wendy suffer and die, which begins the process of his mental breakdown. In the second poem, "Welcome to the Library," Neil is found by Gilver, who serves as an emissary to the titular structure, and guides him there. The Library itself is a mystical place that Gilver describes right from the get-go in this way:

> *This gallery of pain, museum of coping.*
> *Please explore the numerous tomes,*
> *As each contains the experiences*
> *Of your compatriots in agony.*
> *Let them speak to you, influence you;*
> *Each will offer the insights you need*
> *To draw you closer to peace or ruin.*
>
> *Begin wherever you wish, traveler,*
> *And read at the pace you so desire.*
> *Each story will speak to you honestly*
> *And reveal more of human misery.*
> *Stay as long as you require for clarity.*
> *Interact, live, learn, grow through them;*
> *Embrace the panic and obsession,*
> *As you travel, book by book by book.*

This depiction of the Library is one that is central to understanding the theme of pain in the narrative. It is already laid out here that the Library, then, is a place where the stories of those who have suffered are chronicled.

As Neil begins reading the eleven Books that comprise the main portion of the text, he encounters a sort of spirit in each. In relation to the theme, each of these characters has suffered in some way: the Mortician grieves his dead wife, the Clockmaker finds out that he has months left to live, the Degenerate is abandoned by his wife and son, the Child is terrified after having a nightmare, the Farmer battles a monster, the Captive is kidnapped and held in an unknown prison, the Manager loses all her material possessions unexpectedly, the male Twin is betrayed by people he trusted, the female Twin anticipates the inevitable suffering of her brother and is despairing over his choices, the Lover has a lengthy panic attack and is rejected passive-aggressively by the one he loves most, and the Traitor is overtaken by guilt. Each of these manifestations of pain is meant to be a comprehensive survey of all the ills that plague humanity.

On the most surface of reading levels, each of these pains stands as the character's own for what it is (Cuddon 727). However, the Library contains more than eleven different individual pains, as evidenced by the numerous books inside it. So why were these ones chosen for Neil to read? If we look at them on the figurative reading level, these pains are only a glimpse into a larger scope. For example, the Captive's imprisonment may be likened to all forms of shame, not just captivity. The Farmer faces a literal devil;

however this also represents the struggle against any opposing force including inner struggles. The Traitor experiences extreme guilt due to her romantic affair, but guilt, regret, or a strong enough feeling of failure in some way can also come from lying, stealing, not doing something right, or any number of wrongs. The Clockmaker is in mental turmoil because he cannot solve the problem of his dying, but it could really be any life circumstances that cannot be changed that can cause such distress. In this way, the sufferings of the Book characters could in fact stand for all different kinds of pain that humans can endure, comprising an entire spectrum of negative emotions.

On the flipside, just as each of the characters suffers, so too does each of them manage his or her pain in different ways. This is meant to showcase the various ways that humans learn to deal with their individual sufferings, constructs generally known as coping mechanisms (Barlow and Durand 18). Neil has a unique way of dealing with his pain that doesn't necessarily cope, but erases the pain involved, as evidenced in the final stanzas of the story. However, each of the characters in the Books has a respective way of coping as well: the Mortician lives under extreme delusion, the Clockmaker focuses heavily on work and produces artworks through sublimation, the Degenerate escapes with alcohol and gambling, the Child seeks comfort in the arms of his mother, the Farmer adapts and faces his opposition head on, the Captive gives up and does nothing and develops a variant of Stockholm Syndrome in the process, the Manager bullies others to make herself feel better, the male Twin enacts vengeance, the female Twin self-mutilates, the Lover chooses the denial of his counterpart's apathy, and the Traitor commits suicide.

Just like with the negative emotions, the pains, each of the methods of coping can literally only stand for itself. However, on the metaphorical level, they too are a survey of most of, if not all, of the different methods in which people manage their own strife. For example, the female Twin's methods of self-mutilation, biting and cutting, are not the only kind, nor does self-harm necessarily have to be physical in nature (i.e. placing oneself intentionally in emotionally harmful situations). The Child seeks his mother's embrace, but this comfort-seeking could also be in the form of a friend, other family member, or significant other. The Degenerate's form of escapism is alcohol and gambling; however, immersion into worlds of stories, movies, or video games could also be forms of escapism, as it only requires the removal of the harmful stimulus for something more favorable (Barlow and Durand 18). You could say the Captive simply gives up, but her sympathy for and justification of her imprisonment is not unlike the frightful acceptance of a spouse or child in an abusive or unhealthy situation. The Mortician employs a caricatural and extreme form of reaction-formation, believing or acting in a way that is the opposite of reality; however, there are more common ways this is used by people (Barlow and Durand 19). In a way similar to the pains, readers should be able to identify, on some level, with a given character or characters based on their reactions and pain/stress management. You should be able to ask yourself, with regards to both pain and coping, "who am I in this story," and come up with an answer that leads to greater self-discovery at best, and greater appreciation of the text at least.

Neil, based upon his role as the protagonist and main character, endures at length another form of pain that is at the forefront of this theme as well: uncertainty. The fact that the narrative follows from the point of view of Neil highly implies that this pain is meant to be placed on a podium and presented to the audience in full; though this does not necessarily mean it is the objective, or even subjective, worst pain among the characters. Throughout the entire story, Neil references this pain of uncertainty, as his quest in the Library, and his reason for leafing through so many of its books, hinges on his inability to determine a coping mechanism and the lack of knowledge about what his immediate future holds. The spotlight of the book is on the destructive power of uncertainty for a reason: the reader is meant to feel and understand the gravity of how horrible uncertainty can be. By our very natures, humans have a need for control and order; it is an evolutionary survival skill that is part of our basic functioning (Franken 360). Therefore the disruption of this is very often uncomfortable at best, and downright painful at worst. This is one of the most prominent miseries showcased in this book and almost a theme in its own right. It is personified in Neil, a protagonist who grapples with it in one of its worst forms.

There is another character not mentioned in this section thus far who plays a pivotal role in the story, yet is unique from the others: Wendy. She is neither one of the eleven Book characters, nor is she considered to be a main character, since the story is told from the point of view of Neil and she exits the story after the first poem. Yet Wendy herself experiences arguably the worst pain out of all the characters in the narrative. In addition, it is through Wendy's suffering that Neil begins his downward spiral that leads him to and through the Library and eventual mental breakdown. Why is it then that her own point of view is absent from the majority of the narrative? The reason for this is not to demean her role, as I've already stated that her pain is arguably the worst. This story is Neil's though to tell as he is the protagonist and the events of the story are told through his eyes. As such, Wendy's own story is beyond the scope of this book. In some ways, the absence of this focus almost makes a statement that Wendy's pain is too great, too horrific, to be contained within this text. However, the lack of focus on Wendy is simply because this is not the spotlight of the book, as it is on Neil and the Book characters and, to a lesser degree, Gilver. This being said, she should not be overlooked entirely as she has her own role to play in the book, from a purely literary standpoint, as a catalyst for Neil's own journey.

Just as in the real world though, in the narrative, the pain and its relief is not contained into the metaphorically bound boxes that this story lays out. In some cases and in some ways, the experiences, in both pain and reaction, of the respective Book characters overlap. For example, both the Lover and the Degenerate experience rejection as part of their misery, but the latter's was active while the former's was more passive-aggressive. In addition to this notion, it is also highly plausible to glean more than one form of pain from a Character's poem. For example, both the Lover and the female Twin feel great disappoint, the former for his girlfriend and the latter for her brother, in addition to the main hurt that is being exemplified in their poems.

This is meant, from a poetic standpoint, to showcase the reality that we as people don't always feel one type of hurt or one emotion at once; sometimes there are interlaying shades of feelings, both dark and reaction-causing. In addition, this methodology is also not meant to imply that these specific pains lead to these reactions, but instead to showcase all of the respective constructs in a succinct way. As such, if we combine all of the general methods and conceivable combinations of pain and coping that each of the characters, including Neil, employ, they create an effective microcosm of the different ways humans both feel pain and manage it. This is the central theme of *In the Library*.

"There is no choice in life…"

A secondary theme of the narrative would be the construct of Fate, or destiny. This is the idea that all factors in life are predetermined by unknown, supernatural forces and beyond the control of mortal beings (Jung 20). This concept is mentioned numerous times, by characters who believe that their own tragedies were unavoidable. For example, in both the beginning and the end respectively of "Inevitable," the Child imparts to Neil that:

>
> *What is found in the shadows,*
> *Even if unwanted, is inevitable.*

And that:

> *Even a child's tears,*
> *Can't cleanse a fallen destiny.*

These lines showcase the Child's view that his dream was prophetic and that what occurred in it will happen in reality, although the dream itself is rich in symbolism. He is not the only character that feels this way, either. The Clockmaker proclaims that "Fate moves and reacts" and that he was "bullied by Fate," the Farmer speaks of adapting rather than "fighting Fate," the Twins both reference "tools of Fate" and the female Twin claims that "Fate is crueler than [they] knew," and the Traitor notes that "Fate thrives itself on madness." Numerous other times the reference to there not being any choice is rendered as well, which is ironic considering Neil wishes so strongly to choose his path throughout the story. Throughout the journey, the reader sees that the idea that each of the events within the Library was predetermined is highly implied, if not directly stated.

More importantly, in almost every instance, "Fate" is capitalized. Only characters, named or otherwise, are capitalized throughout the poems, so why would an abstract construct such as fate be treated as such? This is done to convey the idea that Fate is in fact a character that is at work in the characters' stories. Rather than being a passive force that exists only as an idea, it is instead suggested that Fate the character is responsible for such events as the Child's "Inevitable" future, the Clockmaker's untimely demise, the Farmer's epilogue after the fight, and the male Twin's imprisonment. In fact, the reason the Child imparts this notion to Neil is to allow for him to blame Fate for the Brutes' assault on Wendy, a notion that he does ponder for a time. Whether Fate is a deity, as sometimes depicted in mythology, or an abstract principality is not relevant (Jung 45). What is relevant is that denoting Fate as a character highlights its importance to the narrative. Death and Time receive similar designations and personifications from the Mortician and Clockmaker respectively for the same reason.

"And embraced the bliss of insanity..."

A third and final important theme is the collective notion of pathology and deconstruction. This is meant in terms of the content of the poem, although the element is certainly the key to understanding the form. It should be stated up front that not all of the characters are mentally compromised, as utilizing coping mechanisms to help to alleviate or lessen the effects of negative emotions is a completely normal function of the human psyche (Barlow and Durand 18). For example, the Clockmaker's use of sublimation, the Lover's form of denial, and the Degenerate's escapism are somewhat common coping mechanisms that many people go through, normally and healthily, at stressful times of life (Barlow and Durand 19). That being said, there are many behaviors executed by the various characters that could be seen as abnormal, disturbing, immoral, or psychopathological. More importantly, these behaviors are actually portrayed as either advantageous or righteous.

For example, in this excerpt from "Afterlife," the Mortician develops psychotic symptoms after the car accident that killed his wife:

> *I carried her home in espousal arms,*
> *And took care of her every day.*
> *We talked and embraced, as lovers should;*
> *No darkness could take that from us.*
>
> *Though life wasn't exactly the same,*
> *I was overjoyed our story was set.*
> *Sometimes she was silent, as was I;*

The strongest delusion, a strange belief that is not held by most of a given society, is that he carries his wife home, believing that she is still alive (Barlow and Durand 486). She is embalmed, so the delusion is able to be kept alive, pun not intended. Moreover, the fact that she is sometimes silent indicates that she is sometimes not; sometimes, she speaks. This is clearly a hallucination on the part of the speaker because his wife is dead; clearly, she is unable to speak. In addition, the fact that it is noted that he is sometimes silent highly implies possible slight catatonic behavior. All of these symptoms, combined with the extremely sudden and brief onset, could easily indicate a diagnosis of schizophreniform or other related psychotic disorder (Barlow and Durand 486). Most people would consider this to be a bad thing; however, the character himself seems extremely happy, so much so that he "laughed at Death." Neil even points out in the subsequent proem that he is happy so he cannot judge him. The reader can then infer that insanity, although on the surface apparently wrong, may actually not be such a terrible thing. This is consistent with this theme of psychopathology.

Most of the Book characters undergo varying levels of anomaly. The female Twin self-mutilates, which is clearly not a healthy way of coping, the male Twin lashes out in revenge, which is fine for himself, but illegal and immoral, the Lover is in stark denial, and the Traitor is dead. However, in a relative way, each of them has found some semblance of happiness. Could we objectively say that the Captive dealt with her situation? No, because she is still imprisoned. But she has found minor comfort in her notion of having taken the moral high ground, as evidenced by her final smile. A discussion on ethics aside, the point is that subjective happiness has been found in all but one of the Book characters: The Degenerate. At the beginning of his poem, he indicates that he is "unlike the others." This is not because he is the sanest, his own problems of alcohol use disorder (alcoholism) and gambling addiction, are clinically diagnosable psychological disorders (Barlow and Durand 402, 433). However, he is the only character that is not subjectively happy by the end of the poem. This is primarily done to show another element of chaos: that the character you would expect to be happy, the one who dopes on drugs of numerous kinds, is not.

The single most important aspect of this point, however, can be exemplified by the main character himself. Neil, as he is first shown in the narrative, is at the happiest point in his life now that his "dream was [his], fulfilled at last." However after the poem's titular trauma, he begins a descent into madness because he is unable to successfully manage what he has seen and felt. This is meant to be seen as a progression, as numerous times in the proems and dialogues, particularly in the last two Book poems, "Word of Healing" and "A Final Dream for Treason," he admits that his mental status is dwindling fast. In the final poem, "Paradise Onward," he at last undergoes a complete mental breakdown and extreme fit of laughter, coupled with amnesia:

The ending,

it is there, or not,

Ha,

  only laughter

    consumes me,
Each sound, ha, loosing away,

These memories,   my pain

   this life,

This final reaction of Neil, which ultimately leads him to walk away from the Library and Wendy's body, could easily be classified clinically as dissociative amnesia, a disorder usually brought on by trauma that leaves the person with an inability to remember important information or memories about the self (Barlow and Durand 198). At best, it could also be categorized as an extreme, caricatural form of suppression, the mind's natural tendency to unconsciously block out or forget painful memories (Barlow and Durand 18). Either way, clearly Neil is not in a sound state of mind, having left his dead lover's body on the ground and not even caring; however, he claims that he "has finally found peace/ and walk[s] onward to a bright horizon." From an objective standpoint, did he make the right call? No, most probably not, but in his insanity, he has found happiness, so it is not a relevant question.

This mode of Neil's descent into insanity is reflected in the form as well. In this work, the first poem contains all stanzas of eight lines each. This is consistent throughout the entire work; the patterned repeating of eight-lined stanzas is held in every poem. However, as the narrative progresses, the stanzas appear less consistent. This is because the original stanzas of eight are broken into smaller pieces. This is meant to simulate the deconstruction of order, from formal stanzas, to "broken" stanzas, but the original eight is always the same. For example, lines can always be grouped into eight, but the stanzas may appear as two quatrains, or a couplet and a sestet, or a triplet and a quintet, or any combination thereof (Johnson 3). This apparent "breaking apart" becomes more frequent as the narrative goes on. The reason for the format being so chaotic is specifically to reflect Neil's own mind as it "breaks apart."

As an example, notice the construction of this stanza from the very beginning of "Trauma," the first poem:

> *We'd walked these paths many times*
> *Over the course of many joyous years.*
> *This venture was no different, I thought;*
> *We crossed flora, blooming as our lives;*
> *For though the sun set on this day,*
> *Ours never would, I believed staunchly.*
> *Blessed to walk, hand and arm*

Intertwined as dreams and life.

Notice how it is a simple construction of eight lines. Now see the construction here in the seventh poem, "The Farmer's Destiny":

I panted, grateful for a life preserved.
And the villagers emerged from their homes,
Now that the Fiend was defeated.

They heralded me their hero:
A brave warrior in turbulent times.
They gave me gold, a champion's prize,
And glory, his undying jewel,
Thus the legend had begun.

Rather than a single stanza of eight, it is instead a stanza of three and a stanza of five. Two poems later, in "Infliction (Volume Two)," the form breaks apart even more:

You told me, you'd make amends,
To protect, like you always have.
But instead you gave up even more:
Your own freedom in exchange for lives.
There is no justice in such a vengeance,

On either side, the good or the evil.
You received your peace and reward
At a price we all had to pay.

By this stage, there are three stanzas taken from an original eight: three, three and two. Finally, in the final poem, the deconstruction is complete:

I can choose,

        this Book,

                my own,

No choice,

        ha, only reaction,

But the ending,

        blank and empty,

I don't care,

        not anymore,

The ending,

        it is there, or not,

Ha,

        only laughter

                consumes me,

Each sound, ha, loosing away,

These memories,   my pain

        this life,

In the end, even the lines themselves are broken apart, although the template of eight remains. Thus, Neil completes his mental breakdown; however, after this event, the final stanza is back to normal, indicating that he is no longer in distress.

While this is the general pattern that occurs within the narrative, there are also specific instances of the "broken" format. Neil and all of the other Book characters all suffer from some form of madness, therefore instances where this is strongly evident harbor the chaotic format as well. For example, during the titular scene during "Trauma," the words in lines appear to be scattered in a seemingly random pattern. This is meant to imitate and escalate the terrifying events that are transpiring. In other cases, such as during the "Infliction" poems, stanzas in moments of extreme panic and suffering are broken apart to mimic this notion. However, no matter the situation, event, or thought process that is occurring, the combination of lines will always add up to stanzas of eight. The reason for this is to demonstrate that even among chaos, there is always some semblance of order. This is the trademark format of *In the Library* and a manifestation of the freedom and juxtaposition of chaos and order that free verse brings to poetry (Kirby 196).

"True misery thrives in the gray…"

While not an actual theme per say, the usage of symbols, allusions, metaphors, and other figures of speech are key to the construction of *In the Library*. Indeed, figurative language in general is trademark of all poetry and one of things that makes it stand out the most from other literary forms (Gwynn 17). The use of these literary constructs is not eluded in this narrative and indeed some of the symbolism and metaphors drawn are vital to truly understanding the work. There are different levels of reading, literal, metaphorical, and critical, and the first is simply understood as the contents of the story. However, as the reader delves down deeper and reads into the next level, different images and meanings begin to appear.

For example, there a number of symbols that are highly prevalent within the narrative. One such is wind, which is a known and ancient symbol of life and "the spirit of the universe" (Cooper 192). In the story, whenever there is wind, there is life, and when there is not, there is some kind of death, either metaphorical or a lack of reality. In the beginning of the story, when Neil and Wendy walk happily, there is certainly wind:

> *A cooling wind soothed the earth*
> *In this city of ours, a truest home.*

This signifies that there is an abundance of life, including metaphorical life, meaning that there is joy and prosperity. Soon after the titular trauma is inflicted, however, the wind is noticeably absent:

> *I could not hear a single sound;*
> *No wind across this godless world,*
> *No breath from her broken body.*

Now that Neil is in a state of desolation, the wind has ceased, signifying that life and love have left him alone and beaten. Similarly, there is no wind when Neil enters the Library, empty inside and about to embark on his quest for peace. By the end, of course, he does find it:

> *I simply lie here on the grass,*
> *No buildings, no lights, no souls.*
> *Just myself, the wind flowing past.*

Once Neil has found the peace he so desperately searched for and left the Library, the wind resumes again. This not only signifies his return to the outside world, but also that there is life within him once again.

Another important symbol throughout *In the Library* is one of its main characters himself: Gilver, "the shadowy guide." Gilver has an important role to play, which on the surface level, appears to be just that. However, if the reader looks at Gilver on a deeper reading level, the significance becomes apparent. Gilver is a crow, a special looking crow, but one such bird nonetheless. In the Japanese culture, the crow is both the symbol for misfortune and messengers (Cooper 47). The character serves as both of these to Neil, being the messenger of the Library and guiding him there, as well as signaling his great misfortune. In addition, the crow is the symbol for death and carrion in the Hebrew tradition, which ties in with the wind imagery used for life and death in Neil's life (Cooper 47). Gilver's depiction as a crow is not the only thing important about him though; his name also bears significance. Gilver, the name, is simply the rearrangement of Virgil, the man who guides Dante through both Hell and Purgatory in Dante the writer's *Divine Comedy*. This is an allusion to the great epic and one that links Gilver's guidance to and through the Library to Virgil, strengthening the imagery.

Of course, wind and crows aren't the only symbols and allusions in the narrative; there are a vast number of them. From the reference to the traditional folk song *The House of the Rising Sun* in "Degenerate," to the numerous Biblical allusions in "Infliction (Volume One)," the figurative language enhances the work and allows the reader to see deeper meanings, if he or she chooses to look into those multiple reading levels of course. The Library itself is a symbol for the vast knowledge that mankind has amassed and contains both the potential for answers and knowledge, and the exploration of pain and all of the human experience. Some of the symbols and imagery, which is an important rhetorical device, are meant to be enigmatic and mysterious; this adds to the feel of the story as well (Gwynn 16). In poetry, the meanings can be numerous and various and therefore, there will always be more meanings to make and find.

"But these shadows will haunt all forms…"

The three major themes and related literary constructs above have been laid out, but they are far from all of the components that make up *In the Library*. The beautiful thing about poetry is that it can mean so many different things to so many different people, not just the implied reader. While certainly there is a message that the author intended to present, that is not the only message, nor should it be. In a sense, a poem or collection of poems has no real relevance to the world unless it is read, thus placing a huge amount of importance on the readers themselves (Siegel 10). Of course it exists as a physical object, but it is not relevant to anything unless it is read, and read multiple times. This implies that the reader, in fact, has an active role in determining the meaning of a poem or poems; the reader then has power (Maynard 300).

In the context of *In the Library*, the free verse format gives it extra freedom for interpretation because this form in general is meant to be read openly for all; its lack of a standard measure allows for this (Gwynn 33). This opens up the world of poetry to anyone who is willing to take the time to read it. Thus poetry is not simply for the elite; it is for all of humanity. Each reader uses his or her own horizon of expectations, their own frame of reference, to carve their own meanings out of a poem, including these ones (Siegel 10). This is an active process, not a passive one. The reader must take up a work and truly ponder its meaning, thus leading to a true appreciation of the work and how it emotionally impacts their own lives.

As a final note, I encourage all readers to do the same for *In the Library*. I could tell you the other notable themes in the work, the meanings of all the allusions and symbols, and other points, but I will not. It is time for me, the author, to take a step back and leave the reader to begin his or her own journey through the text. Gain whatever insights you can and hopefully this will impact your lives, for better or for worse. Mingle with the characters, embrace the scenes, and through staunch reading, may you glean a response fitting the text, thus leading to a proper transactional analysis (Siegel 10). Ask yourself numerous questions that may bring you to a greater understanding of life and the darkness that surrounds all of us, as Neil himself did. May you never join the Library, but may you learn from its tomes, and be inspired and moved in some way. I, the author, fade to black; the time for the reader, the time for the Library, is now.

Works Cited

Alighieri, Dante. *The Divine Comedy*. Trans. H. F Carey. Google Books, 2014. E-Book file.

The Animals. "The House of the Rising Sun." *The Animals*. MGM, 1964.

Barlow, David H., and Mark V. Durand. *Abnormal Psychology: An Integrative Approach,*
    Seventh Edition. Stamford, CT: Cengage Learning, 2012. Print.

"Classics: E. E. Cummings." *Hello Poetry*. N.p., n.d. Web. Dec. 2014. <http://hellopoetry.com/e-
    e-cummings/>.

Cooper, J. C. *An Illustrated Encyclopedia of Traditional Symbols*. London: Thames And
    Hudson, 1978. Print.

Cuddon, J. A. *Dictionary of Literary Terms and Literary Theory*. Ed. C. E Preston. London,
    England: Penguin Books, 1998. Print.

Franken, Robert E. *Human Motivation, Sixth Edition*. Belmont, CA: Wadsworth, Cengage
    Learning, 2007. Print.

Gwynn, R. S. *Poetry: A Pocket Anthology, 4th Ed.* Penguin
Academics, 2005. Print.
Holcombe, John. "Aesthetics." Textetc. 1 Jan. 2007. Web. 27
Oct. 2014.
        <http://www.textetc.com/theory/aesthetics.html>.

Johnson, Burges. *New Rhyming Dictionary and Poets'
Handbook*. New York: Harper And Row,
        2001. Print.

Jung, Carl G. *Psychology and Alchemy*. Princeton, New
Jersey: Princeton University Press,
        1968. Print.

Kirby, H. T. *The Origins of Free Verse*. University Of Michigan
Press, 1998. Print.

Maynard, John. *Literary Intention, Literary Interpretation,
and Readers*. Ontario, Canada:
        Broadview Press, 2009. Print.

New American Bible. St. Joseph edition. Catholic Book
Publishing Corp., 2001. Print

Nichol, Bp. *Art Facts: A Book of Contexts*. Tucson, Arizona:
Chax Press, 1990. Print.

Pink Floyd. *Dark Side of the Moon*. Abbey Road Studios, 1973.

Siegel, Kristi. "Introduction to Modern Literary Theory." Mount
Mary College, Jan. 2006. Web.

Dec. 2014.
<http://www.kristisiegel.com/theory.htm#reception>.

Acknowledgments

There is not a doubt in my mind that I would have been unable to craft this work without the help of numerous, generous people in my life. Firstly, I would like to thank Dr. Francis Tobienne Jr., the Virgil to my Dante, and without whom I would have been lost and unfocused. I would also like to thank Dr. Barbara Jolley, for providing unique insights and advice that truly made this project what is it today.

I am deeply grateful for my family: my Mother, for always having an open door and loving heart for me; my Father, for teaching what it means to be a true hero and for making me laugh even when it's hardest; my cousin Nikki, who is always eager to support me with kind words and the sagest of advice, and, of course, the rest of my family, for always being there for me in ways I could write pages on. I am grateful, too, for all my friends: AJ, Rick, Zach(s), and Jacob, my brothers in arms; Sean, Dakota, and all my mates I've met in the card game community, for helping to keep me sane amidst chaotic times and supporting me along the way; and for all those who've inspired me, both near and far, named and unknown, for walking this path of life with me.

I would like to extend my gratitude to a close friend and advisor, Father Henry Riffle, for offering me support and spiritual guidance throughout my journey both during and before this project; and for Kyle Cormier, for his awesome and elegant cover image, which without, would leave this external book bland and unappealing.

Lastly, and most importantly of all, I want to thank with all my heart, my King, the Lord of all the Universe, for strengthening me every day and helping all things fall into place, and my Queen, Kristiann, for encouraging and believing in me always, standing strong through all darkness and sharing in the brightest of joys. Both have helped me to become the person I am today and inspire me every day to be the best person I can be.

About the Author

James W. A. was born and raised in the Tampa Bay area in Florida and now lives just outside Kansas City, Missouri. After graduating from the University of South Florida, St. Petersburg's Honors College, he published his first book, *In the Library*, in 2015 and second book, *Desolation and Epiphany*, in 2023. Since then, he has honed his ever-evolving, contemporary style, both creatively and as a professional content writer. While moving away from the dark subjects of younger days, James W. A. seeks to use his experiences, joys, sorrows, and wonders he sees in the world around him to lead others to truth and beauty and share meaningful stories to last the ages.

Thejameswa.com
Instagram: @thejameswa